# THE ORDER OF MASS

(The Ordinary Form of the Roman Rite)

Latin and English

# Contents

INTRODUCTORY RITES .................................................................5

THE LITURGY OF THE WORD ........................................................8

THE LITURGY OF THE EUCHARIST ............................................12

Dismissal ...................................................................................26

A Guide to the Pronunciation of Latin.........................................28

# INTRODUCTORY RITES

When the Entrance Chant is concluded,
the Priest and the faithful, standing, sign themselves with
the Sign of the Cross, while the Priest, facing the people, says:

| | |
|---|---|
| In nómine Patris, et Fílii, et Spíritus Sancti. | In the name of the Father, and of the Son, and of the Holy Spirit. |

The people reply:

| | |
|---|---|
| Amen. | Amen. |

Then the Priest, extending his hands, greets the people, saying:

| | |
|---|---|
| Dominus Vobiscum. | The Lord be with you. |

The people respond:

| | |
|---|---|
| Et cum spiritu tuo. | And with your spirit. |

Then follows the Penitential Act, to which the Priest invites the faithful, saying:

| | |
|---|---|
| Fratres, agnoscámus peccáta no·stra, ut apti simus ad sacra mystéria celebránda. | Brethren (brothers and sisters), let us acknowledge our sins, and so prepare ourselves to celebrate the sacred mysteries. |

A brief pause for silence follows.
Then all recite together the formula of general confession:

Confíteor Deo omnipoténti / et vobis, fratres, / quia peccá-vi nimis / cogitatióne, verbo, ópere et omissióne:

*And, striking their breast, they say*

mea culpa, mea culpa, mea máxima culpa.

*Then they continue:*

Ideo precor beátam Maríam semper Vírginem, / omnes Angelos et Sanctos, / et vos, fratres, / oráre pro me ad Dóminum Deum nostrum.

I confess to almighty God and to you, my brothers and sisters, that I have greatly sinned, in my thoughts and in my words, in what I have done and what I have failed to do,

*(striking their breast)*

through my fault, through my fault, through my most grievous fault.

Therefore, I ask blessed Mary ever Virgin, all the Angels and Saints, and you, my brothers and sisters, to pray for me to the Lord our God.

The absolution of the Priest follows:

Misereátur nostri omnípotens Deus et, dimíssis peccátis nostris, perdúcat nos ad vitam ætérnam.

May almighty God have mercy on us, forgive us our sins, and bring us to everlasting life.

The people reply:

Amen.

Amen.

The Kyrie
(Lord, have mercy) invocations follow,
unless they have just occurred in a formula of the Penitential Act.

V. Kyrie, eleison.
R. Kyrie, eleison.
V. Christe, eleison
R. Christe eleison
V. Kyrie, eleison.
R. Kyrie, eleison.

V. Lord, have mercy.
R. Lord, have mercy.
V. Christ, have mercy.
R. Christ, have mercy.
V. Lord, have mercy.
R. Lord, have mercy.

Then, when it is prescribed, the Gloria is sung or said:

Glória in excélsis Deo / et terra pax homínibus bonæ voluntátis. / Laudámus te, benedícimus te, / adorámus te, glorificámus te, / grátias ági-mus tibi / propter magnam glóriam tuam, / Dómine Deus Rex cæléstis, / Deus Pater om-nípotens. / Dómine Fili uni-génite, / Iesu Christe, / Dómi-ne Deus, Agnus Dei, Fílius Pa-tris, / qui tollis peccáta mun- di, / miserére nobis; / qui tollis peccáta mundi, / súscipe de-precatiónem nostram. / Qui sedes ad déxteram Patris, / miserére nobis. / Quóniam tu solus Sanctus, / tu solus Dó-minus, / tu solus Altíssimus / Iesu Christe, / cum Sancto Spíritu: / in glória Dei Patris. Amen. / Amen.

Glory to God in the highest, and on earth peace to people of good will. We praise you, we bless you, we adore you, we glorify you, we give you thanks for your great glory, Lord God, heavenly King, O God, almighty Father. Lord Jesus Christ, Only Begotten Son, Lord God, Lamb of God, Son of the Father, you take away the sins of the world, have mercy on us; you take away the sins of the world, receive our prayer; you are seated at the right hand of the Father, have mercy on us. For you alone are the Holy One, you alone are the Lord, you alone are the Most High, Jesus Christ, with the Holy Spirit, in the glory of God the Father. Amen.

When this hymn is concluded, the Priest, with hands joined, says:

Orémus.

Let us pray.

And all pray in silence with the Priest for a moment.

Then the Priest, with hands extended, says the Collect prayer. At the end of which the people acclaim:

Amen.

Amen.

# THE LITURGY OF THE WORD

Then the reader goes to the ambo and reads the first reading,
while all sit and listen.
To indicate the end of the reading, the reader acclaims:

| | |
|---|---|
| Verbum Dómini. | The Word of the Lord. |

All reply:

| | |
|---|---|
| Deo grátias. | Thanks be to God. |

After the First Reading the psalmist or cantor sings or says the Psalm,
with the people making the response.

On Sundays and certain other days there is a second reading.
It concludes with the same responsory as above.
There follows the Alleluia or another chant laid down by the rubrics,
as the liturgical time requires.
Meanwhile, if incense is used,
the Priest puts some into the thurible.

After this, the deacon who is to proclaim the Gospel,
bowing profoundly before the Priest,
asks for the blessing,
saying in a low voice:

| | |
|---|---|
| Iube, domne, benedícere. | Your blessing, Father. |

The Priest says in a low voice:

| | |
|---|---|
| Dóminus sit in corde tuo et in lábiis tuis, ut digne et competénter annúnties Evangélium suum: | May the Lord be in your heart and on your lips that you may proclaim his Gospel worthily and well, |
| in nómine Patris, et Fílii, + et Spíritus Sancti. | in the name of the Father and of the Son + and of the Holy Spirit. |

The deacon signs himself with the Sign of the Cross and replies:

Amen.

Amen.

If, however, a deacon is not present,
the Priest, bowing before the altar, says quietly:

Munda cor meum ac lábia mea,
omnípotens Deus, ut sanctum
Evangélium tuum digne váleam
nuntiáre.

Cleanse my heart and my lips,
almighty God, that I may
worthily proclaim your holy
Gospel.

The deacon, or the Priest, then proceeds to the ambo,
accompanied, if appropriate,
by ministers with incense and candles.

There he says:

Dóminus vobíscum.

The Lord be with you.

The people reply:

Et cum Spíritu tuo.

And with your spirit.

The deacon, or the Priest:

Lectio sancti Evangélii
secun-dum N.

A reading from the holy Gospel
according to N.

and, at the same time,
he makes the Sign of the Cross on the book
and on his forehead, lips, and breast.

The people acclaim:

Glória tibi, Dómine.

Glory to you, O Lord.

At the end of the Gospel, the deacon, or the Priest, acclaims:

Verbum Dómini.

The Gospel of the Lord.

Laus tibi, Christe. | Praise to you, Lord Jesus Christ.

*Then he kisses the book, saying quietly:*

Per evangélica dicta deleántur nostra delícta. | Through the words of the Gospel may our sins be wiped away.

At the end of the homily,
the Symbol or Profession of Faith or Creed,
when prescribed, is sung or said:

Credo in unum Deum, / Pa-trem omnipoténtem, / factó-rem cæli et terræ, / visibilium omnium et invisibilium,/ Et in unum Dominum Iesum Christum,/ Filium Dei unigenitum,/ et ex Patre natum, ante omnia saecula,/ Deum de Deo, lumen de Lumine, / Deum verum de Deo vero,/ genitum, non factum, consubstantialem Patri:/ per quem omnia facta sunt. / Qui propter nos homines et propter nostram salutem descendit de caelis. /

*(All bow during the following two lines:)*

Et incarnatus est de Spiritu Sancto / ex Maria Virgine, et homo factus est. / Crucifixus etiam pro nobis sub Pontio Pilato; / passus et sepultus est, / et resurrexit tertia die, secundem Scripturas, / et ascendit in caelum, sedet ad dexteram Patris. / Et iterum venturus est cum gloria, / iudicare vivos et mortuos, / cuius regni non erit finis. / Et in Spiritum Sanctum, Dominum et vivificantem: / qui ex Patre Filioque procedit. / Qui cum Patre et Filio simul adoratur et conglorificatur: / qui locutus est per prophetas. / Et unam, sanctam, catholicam et apostolicam Ecclesiam. / Confiteor unum baptisma in remissionem peccatorum. / Et exspecto resurrectionem mortuorum, / et vitam venturi saeculi. Amen.

I believe in one God, the Father almighty, maker of heaven and earth, of all things visible and invisible. I believe in one Lord Jesus Christ, the Only Begotten Son of God, born of the Father before all ages. God from God, Light from Light, true God from true God, begotten, not made, consubstantial with the Father; through him all things were made. For us men and for our salvation he came down from heaven,

*(At the words that follow up to and including and became man, all bow.)*

and by the Holy Spirit was incarnate of the Virgin Mary, and became man. For our sake he was crucified under Pontius Pilate, he suffered death and was buried, and rose again on the third day in accordance with the Scriptures. He ascended into heaven and is seated at the right hand of the Father. He will come again in glory to judge the living and the dead and his kingdom will have no end. I believe in the Holy Spirit, the Lord, the giver of life, who proceeds from the Father and the Son, who with the Father and the Son is adored and glorified, who has spoken through the prophets. I believe in one, holy, catholic and apostolic Church. I confess one Baptism for the forgiveness of sins and I look forward to the resurrection of the dead and the life of the world to come. Amen

Then follows the Universal Prayer,
that is, the Prayer of the Faithful or Bidding Prayers.

# THE LITURGY OF THE EUCHARIST

The Priest, standing at the altar, takes the paten with the bread and holds it slightly raised above the altar with both hands, saying in a low voice:

Benedictus es, Dómine, Deus univérsi, quia de tua largitáte accépimus panem, quem tibi offérimus, fructum terræ et ópe-ris mánuum hóminum: ex quo nobis fiet panis vitæ.

Blessed are you, Lord God of all creation, for through your goodness we have received the bread we offer you: fruit of the earth and work of human hands, it will become for us the bread of life.

Then he places the paten with the bread on the corporal. If, however, the Offertory Chant is not sung, the Priest may speak these words aloud; at the end, the people may acclaim:

Benedíctus Deus in sǽcula.

Blessed be God for ever.

The deacon, or the Priest, pours wine
and a little water into the chalice, saying quietly:

Per huius aquæ et vini mystérium eius efficiámur divinitátis consórtes, qui humanitátis nostræ fíeri dignátus est párticeps.

By the mystery of this water and wine may we come to share in the divinity of Christ who humbled himself to share in our humanity.

The Priest then takes the chalice and holds it slightly raised
above the altar with both hands,
saying in a low voice:

| | |
|---|---|
| Benedíctus es, Dómine, Deus univérsi, quia de tua largitáte accépimus vinum, quod tibi offérimus, fructum vitis et óperis mánuum hóminum, ex quo nobis fiet potus spiritális. | Blessed are you, Lord God of all creation, for through your goodness we have received the wine we offer you: fruit of the vine and work of human hands, it will become our spiritual drink. |

Then he places the chalice on the corporal.
If, however, the Offertory Chant is not sung,
the Priest may speak these words aloud;
at the end, the people may acclaim:

| | |
|---|---|
| Benedíctus Deus in sǽcula. | Blessed be God for ever. |

After this, the Priest, bowing profoundly, says quietly:

| | |
|---|---|
| In spíritu humilitátis et in ánimo contríto suscipiámur a te, Dómine; et sic fiat sacrifícium nostrum in conspéctu tuo hódie. ut pláceat tibi, Dómine Deus. | With humble spirit and contrite heart may we be accepted by you, O Lord, and may our sacrifice in your sight this day be pleasing to you, Lord God. |

Then the Priest, standing at the side of the altar,
washes his hands, saying quietly:

| | |
|---|---|
| Lava me, Dómine, ab iniquitá·te mea, et a peccáto meo munda me. | Wash me, O Lord, from my inquity and cleanse me from my sin. |

Standing at the middle of the altar,
facing the people, extending and then joining his hands,
he says:

| | |
|---|---|
| Oráte, fratres: ut meum ac vestrum sacrifícium acceptábile fiat apud Deum Patrem omnipoténtem. | Pray, brethren (brothers and sisters), that my sacrifice and yours may be acceptable to God, the almighty Father. |

The people rise and reply:

Suscípiat Dóminus sacri-fícium / de mánibus tuis / ad laudem et glóriam nómi- nis sui, / ad utilitátem quoque nostram / totiúsque Ecclésiæ suæ sanctæ.

May the Lord accept the sacrifice at your hands for the praise and glory of his name, for our good and the good of all his holy Church.

Then the Priest, with hands extended, says the Prayer over the Offerings, at the end of which the people acclaim:

Amen.

Amen.

V. Dominus Vobi'scum
R. Et cum spi'ritu tuo
V. Sursum Corda
R. Habe'mus ad Do'minum
V. Gra'tias aga'mus Do'mino Deo nostro
R. Dignum et justum est.

V. The Lord be with you.
R. And with your spirit.
V. Lift up your hearts.
R. We lift them up to the Lord.
V. Let us give thanks to the Lord our God.
R. It is right and just.

The Priest, with hands extended, continues the Preface. At the end of the Preface he joins his hands and concludes the Preface with the people, singing or saying aloud:

SANCTUS, Sanctus, Sanctus, Dominus Deus Sabaoth. Pleni sunt caeli et terra gloria tua. Hosanna in excelsis. Benedictus qui venit in nomine Domini. Hosanna in excelsis.

Holy, Holy, Holy Lord God of hosts. Heaven and earth are full of your glory. Hosanna in the highest. Blessed is he who comes in the name of the Lord. Hosanna in the highest.

The Priest, with hands extended, says:

Te ígitur, clementíssime Pa-ter, per Iesum Christum, Fí- lium tuum, Dóminum nostrum, súpplices rogámus ac pétimus, uti accépta hábeas et benedí-cas + hæc dona, hæc múne-ra, hæc sancta sacrifícia illibá-ta, in primis, quæ tibi offérimus pro Ecclésia tua sancta cathóli-ca: quam pacificáre, custodíre, adunáre et régere dignéris toto orbe terrárum: una cum fámu- lo tuo Papa nostro et Antístite nostro N. et ómnibus orthodóxis atque cathólicæ et apostólicæ fídei cultóribus.

To you, therefore, most merciful Father, we make humble prayer and petition through Jesus Christ, your Son, our Lord: that you accept and bless +  these gifts, these offerings, these holy and unblemished sacrifices, which we offer you first of all for your holy catholic Church. Be pleased to grant her peace, to guard, unite and govern her throughout the whole world, together with your servant N. our Pope and N. our Bishop, and all those who, holding to the truth, hand on the catholic and apostolic faith.

Meménto, Dómine, famulórum famularúmque tuarum N. et N. et ómnium circumstántium, quórum tibi fides cógnita est et nota devótio, pro quibus tibi offérimus: vel qui tibi ófferunt hoc sacrifícium laudis, pro se suís- que ómnibus: pro redemptióne animárum suárum, pro spe salú-tis et incolumitátis suæ: tibíque reddunt vota sua ætérno Deo, vi-vo et vero.

Remember, Lord, your servants N. and N. and all gathered here, whose faith and devotion are known to you. For them and all who are dear to them we offer you this sacrifice of praise or they offer it for themselves and all who are dear to them, for the redemption of their souls, in hope of health and well-being, and fulfilling their vows to you, the eternal God, living and true.

Communicántes, et memóriam venerántes, in primis gloriósæ semper Vírginis Maríæ, Genetrícis Dei et Dómini nostri Ie- su Christi: sed et beáti Iose- ph, eiúsdem Vírginis Sponsi, et beatórum Apostolórum ac Mártyrum tuórum, Petri et Pauli, Andréæ, (Iacóbi, Ioánnis, Thomæ, Iacóbi, Philíppi, Bartholomǽi, Matthǽi, Simónis et Thaddǽi: Lini, Cleti, Cleméntis, Xysti, Cornélii, Cypriáni, Laurén-tii, Chrysógoni, Ioánnis et Pau-li, Cosmæ et Damiáni) et óm-nium Sanctórum tuórum; quó-rum méritis precibúsque concé-das, ut in ómnibus protectió-nis tuæ muniámur auxílio. (Per Christum Dóminum nostrum. Amen.)

In communion with those whose memory we venerate, especially the glorious ever-Virgin Mary, Mother of our God and Lord, Jesus Christ, and blessed Joseph, her Spouse, your blessed Apostles and Martyrs, Peter and Paul, Andrew, (James, John, Thomas, James, Philip, Bartholomew, Matthew, Simon and Jude: Linus, Cletus, Clement, Sixtus, Cornelius, Cyprian, Lawrence, Chrysogonus, John and Paul, Cosmas and Damian) and all your Saints: through their merits and prayers, grant that in all things we may be defended by your protecting help. (Through Christ our Lord. Amen.)

Hanc ígitur oblatiónem servitú-tis nostræ, sed et cunctæ famíliæ tuæ, quǽsumus, Dómine, ut pla-cátus accípias: diésque nostros in tua pace dispónas, atque ab ætérna damnatióne nos éripi et in electórum tuórum iúbeas gre-ge numerári. (Per Christum Dó-minum nostrum. Amen.)

Therefore, Lord, we pray: graciously accept this oblation of our service, that of your whole family; order our days in your peace, and command that we be delivered from eternal damnation and counted among the flock of those you have chosen.(Through Christ our Lord. Amen.)

Quam oblatiónem tu, Deus, in ómnibus, quǽsumus, benedíc-tam, adscríptam, ratam, ratio-nábilem, acceptabilémque fáce-re dignéris: ut nobis Corpus et Sanguis fiat dilectíssimi Fílii tui, Dómini nostri Iesu Christi.

Be pleased, O God, we pray, to bless, acknowledge, and approve this offering in every respect; make it spiritual and acceptable, so that it may become for us the Body and Blood of your most beloved Son, our Lord Jesus Christ.

Qui, prídie quam paterétur, accépit panem in sanctas ac venerábiles manus suas, et elevátis óculis in cælum ad te Deum Patrem suum omnipoténtem, tibi grátias agens benedíxit, fregit, dedítque discípulis suis, dicens:

ACCÍPITE ET MANDUCÁTE EX HOC OMNES: HOC EST ENIM COR-PUS MEUM, QUOD PRO VOBIS TRADÉTUR.

On the day before he was to suffer he took bread in his holy and venerable hands, and with eyes raised to heaven to you, O God, his almighty Father, giving you thanks he said the blessing, broke the bread and gave it to his disciples, saying:
TAKE THIS, ALL OF YOU, AND EAT OF IT, FOR THIS IS MY BODY,  WHICH WILL BE GIVEN UP FOR YOU.

He shows the consecrated host to the people,
places it again on the paten, and genuflects in adoration.

Símili modo, postquam cená-tum est, accípiens et hunc præ-clárum cálicem in sanctas ac ve-nerábiles manus suas, item ti-bi grátias agens benedíxit, dedít-que discípulis suis, dicens:

ACCÍPITE ET BÍBITE EX EO OM-NES: HIC EST ENIM CALIX SÁN-GUINIS MEI NOVI ET ÆTÉRNI TE-STAMÉNTI, QUI PRO VOBIS ET PRO MULTIS EFFUNDÉTUR IN RE-MISSIÓNEM PECCATÓRUM. HOC FÁCITE IN MEAM COMMEMORA-TIÓNEM.

In a similar way, when supper was ended, he took this precious chalice in his holy and venerable hands, and once more giving you thanks, he said the blessing and gave the chalice to his disciples, saying:
TAKE THIS, ALL OF YOU, AND DRINK FROM IT, FOR THIS IS THE CHALICE OF MY BLOOD, THE BLOOD OF THE NEW AND ETER NAL COVENANT, WHICH WILL BE POURED OUT FOR YOU AND FOR MANY FOR THE FORGIVENESS OF SINS. DO THIS IN MEMORY OF ME.

The Priest shows the chalice to the people,
places it on the corporal,
and genuflects in adoration.

V. Mysterium Fidei
R. Mortem tu-am annunti-a'mus, Do'mine, et tu-am re-surrecti-o-nem confi-te'mur, donec ve'ni-as.

V. The Mystery of Faith
R. We proclaim your Death, O Lord, and profess your Resurrection until you come again.

Unde et mémores, Dómine, nos servi tui, sed et plebs tua sanc-ta, eiúsdem Christi, Fílii tui, Dómini nostri, tam beátæ passiónis, necnon et ab ínferis resurrectiónis, sed et in cælos gloriósæ ascensiónis: offérimus præcláræ maiestáti tuæ de tuis donis ac datis hóstiam puram, hóstiam sanctam, hóstiam immaculátam, Panem sanctum vitæ ætérnæ et Cálicem salútis perpétuæ.

Therefore, O Lord, as we celebrate the memorial of the blessed Passion, the Resurrection from the dead, and the glorious Ascension into heaven of Christ, your Son, our Lord, we, your servants and your holy people, offer to your glorious majesty from the gifts that you have given us, this pure victim, this holy victim, this spotless victim, the holy Bread of eternal life and the Chalice of everlasting salvation.

Supra quæ propítio ac seréno vultu respícere dignéris: et accépta habére, sícuti accépta habére dignátus es múnera púeri tui iusti Abel, et sacrifícium Patriárchæ nostri Abrahæ, et quod tibi óbtulit summus sacérdos tuus Melchísedech, sanctum sacrifícium, immaculátam hóstiam.

Be pleased to look upon them with serene and kindly countenance, and to accept them, as you were pleased to accept the gifts of your servant Abel the just, the sacrifice of Abraham, our father in faith, and the offering of your high priest Melchizedek, a holy sacrifice, a spotless victim.

Súpplices te rogámus, omnípotens Deus: iube hæc perférri per manus sancti Angeli tui in sublíme altáre tuum, in conspéctu divínæ maiestátis tuæ; ut, quotquot ex hac altáris participatióne sacrosánctum Fílii tui Corpus et Sánguinem sumpsérimus, omni benedictióne cælesti et grátia repleámur. (Per Christum Dóminum nostrum. Amen.)

In humble prayer we ask you, almighty God: command that these gifts be borne by the hands of your holy Angel to your altar on high in the sight of your divine majesty, so that all of us who through this participation at the altar receive the most holy Body and Blood of your Son may be filled with every grace and heavenly blessing. (Through Christ our Lord. Amen.)

Meménto étiam, Dómine, famulórum famularúmque tuárum N. et N., qui nos præcessérunt cum signo fídei, et dórmiunt in somno pacis.

Remember also, Lord, your servants N. and N., who have gone before us with the sign of faith and rest in the sleep of peace.

Ipsis, Dómine, et ómnibus in Christo quiescéntibus, locum refrigérii, lucis et pacis, ut indúlgeas, deprecámur. (Per Christum Dóminum nostrum. Amen.)

Grant them, O Lord, we pray, and all who sleep in Christ, a place of refreshment, light and peace. (Through Christ our Lord. Amen.)

Nobis quoque peccatóribus fámulis tuis, de multitúdine miseratiónum tuárum sperántibus, partem áliquam et societátem donáre dignéris cum tuis sanctis Apóstolis et Martýribus: cum Ioánne, Stéphano, Matthía, Bárnaba, (Ignátio, Alexándro, Marcellíno, Petro, Felicitáte, Perpétua, Agatha, Lúcia, Agnéte, Cæcília, Anastásia) et ómnibus Sanctis tuis: intra quorum nos consórtium, non æstimátor mériti, sed véniæ, quæsumus, largítor admítte. Per Christum Dóminum nostrum.

Per quem hæc ómnia, Dómine, semper bona creas, sanctíficas, vivíficas, benedícis, et præstas nobis.

To us, also, your sinful servants, who hope in your abundant mercies, graciously grant some share and fellowship with your holy Apostles and Martyrs: with John the Baptist, Stephen, Matthias, Barnabas, (Ignatius, Alexander, Marcellinus, Peter, Felicity, Perpetua, Agatha, Lucy, Agnes, Cecilia, Anastasia) and all your Saints: admit us, we beg you, into their company, not weighing our merits, but granting us your pardon, through Christ our Lord. Through whom you continue to make all these good things, O Lord; you make them holy, fill them with life, bless them, and bestow them upon us.

Per ipsum, et cum ipso, et in ipso, est tibi Deo Patri omnipoténti, in unitáte Spíritus Sancti, omnis honor et glória per ómnia sæcula sæculorum.

Through him, and with him, and in him, to you, O God, almighty Father, in the unity of the Holy Spirit, is all honor and glory, for ever and ever.

The people acclaim:

Amen.

Amen.

After the chalice and paten have been set down,
the Priest, with hands joined, says:

| | |
|---|---|
| Præcéptis salutáribus móniti, et divína institutióne formáti, audémus dícere: | At the Savior's command and formed by divine teaching, we dare to say: |

He extends his hands and, together with the people, continues:

| | |
|---|---|
| Pater noster, qui es in caelis: sanctificetur Nomen Tuum; adveniat Regnum Tuum; fiat voluntas Tua, sicut in caelo, et in terra. Panem nostrum cotidianum da nobis hodie; et dimitte nobis debita nostra, sicut et nos dimittimus debitoribus nostris; et ne nos inducas in tentationem; sed libera nos a Malo. | Our Father, who art in heaven, hallowed be thy name; thy kingdom come, thy will be done on earth as it is in heaven. Give us this day our daily bread, and forgive us our trespasses, as we forgive those who trespass against us; and lead us not into temptation, but deliver us from evil. |

With hands extended,
the Priest alone continues, saying:

| | |
|---|---|
| Líbera nos, quǽsumus, Dómine, ab ómnibus malis, da propítius pacem in diébus nostris, ut, ope misericórdiæ tuæ adiúti, et a peccáto simus semper líberi et ab omni perturbatióne secúri: exspectántes beátam spem et advéntum Salvatóris nostri Iesu Christi. · | Deliver us, Lord, we pray, from every evil, graciously grant peace in our days, that, by the help of your mercy, we may be always free from sin and safe from all distress, as we await the blessed hope and the coming of our Savior, Jesus Christ. |

He joins his hands.
The people conclude the prayer, acclaiming:

| | |
|---|---|
| Quia tuum est regnum, / et potéstas, / et glória in sǽcula. | For the kingdom, the power and the glory are yours now and for ever. |

Then the Priest, with hands extended, says aloud:

Dómine Iesu Christe, qui dixísti Apóstolis tuis: Pacem relínquo vobis, pacem meam do vobis: ne respícias peccáta nostra, sed fidem Ecclésiæ tuæ; eám- que secúndum voluntátem tuam pacificáre et coadunáre digneris. Qui vivis et regnas in sǽcula sæculorum.

Lord Jesus Christ, who said to your Apostles: Peace I leave you, my peace I give you, look not on our sins, but on the faith of your Church, and graciously grant her peace and unity in accordance with your will. Who live and reign for ever and ever.

The people reply:

Amen.

Amen.

The Priest, turned towards the people, extending and then joining his hands, adds:

Pax Dómini sit semper vobíscum.

The peace of the Lord be with you always.

The people reply:

Et cum spíritu tuo.

And with your spirit.

Then, if appropriate, the deacon, or the Priest, adds:

Offérte vobis pacem.

Let us offer each other the sign of peace.

And all offer one another a sign,
in keeping with local customs,
that expresses peace, communion, and charity.

The Priest gives the sign of peace to a deacon or minister. Then he takes the host, breaks it over the paten, and places a small piece in the chalice, saying quietly:

Hæc commíxtio Córporis et Sánguinis Dómini nostri Iesu Christi fiat accipiéntibus nobis in vitam ætérnam.

May this mingling of the Body and Blood of our Lord Jesus Christ bring eternal life to us who receive it.

Meanwhile the following is sung or said:

Agnus Dei, qui tollis pecca'ta mundi, misere're nobis.
Agnus Dei, qui tollis pecca'ta mundi, misere're nobis.
Agnus Dei, qui tollis pecca'ta mundi, dona nobis pacem.

Lamb of God, you take away the sins of the world, have mercy on us. Lamb of God, you take away the sins of the world, have mercy on us. Lamb of God, you take away the sins of the world, grant us peace.

Then the Priest, with hands joined, says quietly:

Dómine Iesu Christe, Fili Dei vivi, qui ex voluntáte Patris, cooperánte Spíritu Sancto, per mortem tuam mundum vivificásti: líbera me per hoc sacrosánctum Corpus et Sánguinem tuum ab ómnibus iniquitátibus meis et univérsis malis: et fac me tuis semper inhærére mandátis, et a te numquam separári permíttas.

Lord Jesus Christ, Son of the living God, who by the will of the Father and the work of the Holy Spirit, through your death gave life to the world; free me by this your most holy Body and Blood from all my sins and from every evil; keep me always faithful to your commandments, and never let me be parted from you.

The Priest genuflects, takes the host and,
holding it slightly raised above the paten or above the chalice,
while facing the people, says aloud:

| | |
|---|---|
| Ecce Agnus Dei, ecce qui tollit peccáta mundi. Beáti qui ad cenam Agni vocáti sunt. | Behold the Lamb of God, behold him who takes away the sins of the world. Blessed are those called to the supper of the Lamb. |

And together with the people he adds once:

| | |
|---|---|
| Dómine, non sum dignus, / ut intres sub tectum meum, / sed tantum dic verbo / et sanábitur ánima mea. | Lord, I am not worthy that you should enter under my roof, but only say the word and my soul shall be healed. |

The Priest, facing the altar, says quietly:

| | |
|---|---|
| Corpus Christi custódiat me in vitam ætérnam. | May the Body of Christ keep me safe for eternal life. |

And he reverently consumes the Body of Christ.
Then he takes the chalice and says quietly:

| | |
|---|---|
| Sanguis Christi custódiat me in vitam ætérnam. | May the Blood of Christ keep me safe for eternal life. |

And he reverently consumes the Blood of Christ.

After this, he takes the paten or ciborium
and approaches the communicants.

The Priest raises a host slightly
and shows it to each of the communicants, saying:

| | |
|---|---|
| Corpus Christi. | The Body of Christ. |

The communicant replies:

| | |
|---|---|
| Amen. | Amen. |

The Deacon gives communion from the chalice, saying:

| | |
|---|---|
| Sanguis Christi | The Blood of Christ. |
| Amen. | Amen. |

When the distribution of Communion is over,
the Priest or a deacon or an acolyte
purifies the paten over the chalice
and also the chalice itself.

While he carries out the purification,
the Priest says quietly:

| | |
|---|---|
| Quod ore súmpsimus, Dómine, pura mente capiámus, et de múnere temporáli fiat nobis remédium sempitérnum.ˉ | What has passed our lips as food, O Lord, may we possess in purity of heart, that what has been given to us in time may be our healing for eternity. |

Then, standing at the altar or at the chair
and facing the people, with hands joined,
the Priest says:

| | |
|---|---|
| Orémus. | Let us pray. |

All pray in silence with the Priest for a while,
unless silence has just been observed.

Then the Priest, with hands extended,
says the Prayer after Communion,
at the end of which the people acclaim:

| | |
|---|---|
| Amen. | Amen. |

# Dismissal

The Priest, facing the people and extending his hands, says:

Do'minus Vobiscum. | The Lord be with you.

The Priest blesses the people, saying:

Benedícat vos omnípotens Deus, Pater, et Filius, + et Spíritus Sanctus. | May almighty God bless you: the Father, and the Son, + and the Holy Spirit.

The people reply:

Amen. | Amen.

Then the deacon, or the Priest himself, with hands joined and facing the people, says:

Ite, missa est. | Go forth, the Mass is ended.

The people reply:

Deo gratias. | Thanks be to God

"Particular law remaining in force, the use of the Latin language is to be preserved in the Latin rites." (Vatican II, Sacrosanctum Concilium, n. 36)

"Steps should be taken so that the faithful may also be able to say or to sing together in Latin those parts of the Ordinary of the Mass which pertain to them." (Vatican II, Sacrosanctum Concilium, n. 50)

"Pastors of souls should take care that besides the vernacular 'the faithful may also be able to say or sing together in Latin those parts of the Ordinary of the Mass which pertain to them.'" (Sacred Congregation of Rites, Musicam sacram (1967), n. 47)

"The Roman Church has special obligations towards Latin, the splendid language of ancient Rome, and she must manifest them whenever the occasion presents itself." (John Paul II, Dominicae cenae (1980), n. 10)

"Mass is celebrated either in Latin or in another language, provided that liturgical texts are used which have been approved according to the norm of law. Except in the case of celebrations of the Mass that are scheduled by the ecclesiastical authorities to take place in the language of the people, Priests are always and everywhere permitted to celebrate Mass in Latin." (Congregation for Divine Worship and the Discipline of the Sacraments, Redemptionis Sacramentum (2004), n. 112)

"I ask that future priests, from their time in the seminary, receive the preparation needed to understand and to celebrate Mass in Latin, and also to use Latin texts and execute Gregorian chant; nor should we forget that the faithful can be taught to recite the more common prayers in Latin, and also to sing parts of the liturgy to Gregorian chant." (Benedict XVI, Sacramentum caritatis (2007), n. 62) Latin text taken from the Missale Romanum, editio typica tertia emendata of 2008.

# A Guide to the Pronunciation of Latin

Vowels:

    1.A, E, I, O and (normally, but see iii below) U are pronounced as in Italian or Spanish, that is more or less like the vowels in father, red, feet, for and moon respectively.

    2.Y which is rare and mainly in Greek words) is pronounced the same as Latin i.

    3.After q and after ng if another vowel follows, u is pronounced like an English w; for example: quam (kwahm), sanguis (sahngwees).

    4.Æ and Œ (sometimes printed as ae and oe) are both pronounced the same as Latin e.

    5.Otherwise, if two vowels occur together, each is pronounced separately. The common combination AU, therefore, sounds like the English ow in cow.

Which vowel to stress:

    1.in words of two syllable, stress is always on the first vowel.

    2.In words of three or more syllables, the rules are more complicated. Helpful texts show stress by putting an acute accent on the stressed vowel; e.g. sǽcula sæculórum.

The consonants:

Double consonants should be clearly sounded and pronounced double, as in Italian.

(Consonants not shown below are given their normal English pronunciation.)

    C
- Before e, æ, œ, I or y as English ch in church. Note that CC before the same vowels is pronounced t-chas, for example, in ecce (et-cheh).
- For the combinations SC and XC, see below.
- Otherwise Latin C is like English k.

    CH
- Latin CH is always like English k.

    G
- Before e, æ, œ, I or y as English g in ginger.
- GN has the sound given to these letters in French agneau and the Italian signor, that is similar to the English ny in canyon
- Otherwise Latin G is like English g in get.

    H
- H is pronounced like k in the two words nihil (neekeel) and mihi (meekee) and their compounds. (In medieval times these words were often written "nichil" and "michi").

| | |
|---|---|
| | • In all other cases Latin H is silent as in English hour. |
| J | • Latin J is always as in Hallelujah - the sound that is usually spelt in English with a y as in yes, yellow etc.<br>Note: before the Renaissance both I and J were written the same way; there has been a tendency in recent times to write this consonant as I |
| R | • Latin R should always be sounded. Strictly it should be trilled as in Italian or in Scots. Care shoud be taken NOT to pronounce Latin ER, IR and UR like the er as commonly pronounced in English herd; the two sounds should be given their own proper sounds as they are, for example, in Scots English. |
| SC | • Before e, æ, œ, I or y as English sh in shed.<br>• Before any other sounds, Latin SC is like English sk.<br>(Latin S is otherwise like English so or rose) |
| TH | • Latin TH is always as in Thomas. |
| TI | • before a vowel (except when it comes after after S, T or X) is pronounced 'tsee'; for example propítia(proPEEtsee-ah).<br>• Otherwise Latin TI is like English tee. |
| XC | • Before e, æ, œ, I or y as English ksh sound in bikeshed; for example excélsis (ek-SHELL-sees)<br>• Before any other sounds, Latin XC is like English xc in excuse.<br>(Latin X is otherwise like English fox) |
| Z | • Latin Z is always as in English dz in adze. |

Made in the USA
Middletown, DE
19 June 2020

10340414R00018